BRITISH SUBMARINES
OF WORLD WAR ONE

Paul J. Kemp

ARMS AND
ARMOUR

▲2

2. 'E' boats manoeuvring at Harwich alongside their depot ships in the early morning. The minelayer *E34*, on the right was the twenty-ninth and last 'E' class submarine to be sunk during the war. She is believed to have been mined around 20 July 1918: the body of her CO, Lt R. I. Pulleyne, was later washed ashore on the West Fresian Islands. Sixty British submarines were sunk and 1,190 submariners lost their lives during the First World War.

3. HM Submarine *A1*, the first all-British submarine. *A1* was a single-hull, single-screw design powered by a petrol engine – in fact an advanced version of the five Holland boats built under licence at Barrow. *A1* was also the first British submarine casualty, being sunk on 18 March 1904 in collision with the *Berwick Castle*; she was raised but never recommissioned. She was followed by twelve more, the last eight being built to a modified design. *A13*, the last of the class, was the first British submarine to be fitted with a diesel engine.

▼3

INTRODUCTION

First published in Great Britain in 1990 by Arms and Armour Press, Artillery House, Artillery Row, London SW1P 1RT.

Distributed in the USA by Sterling Publishing Co. Inc., 387 Park Avenue South, New York, NY 10016–8810.

Distributed in Australia by Capricorn Link (Australia) Pty. Ltd, P.O. Box 665, Lane Cove, New South Wales 2066, Australia.

British Library Cataloguing in Publication Data
Kemp, Paul
British submarines of World War One.
1. Great Britain. Royal Navy. Submarines, history
I. Title   II. Series
623.8'257'0941
ISBN 1-85409-010-0

Line illustrations by David Hill.

Designed and edited by DAG Publications Ltd. Designed by David Gibbons; edited by Roger Chesneau; layout by Cilla Eurich; typeset by Ronset Typesetters Ltd, Darwen, Lancashire, and Typesetters (Birmingham) Ltd, Warley, West Midlands; camerawork by M&E Reproductions, North Fambridge, Essex; printed and bound in Great Britain by The Alden Press, Oxford.

At the beginning of the Great War the Royal Navy had seventy-four submarines in commission – the largest number of any of the Great Powers. Yet the Admiralty had little idea of what to do with their submarines, which had been acquired more as a result of pressure from abroad than because of any enthusiasm for this new naval weapon. Indeed, the attitude of the Royal Navy towards the submarine was decidedly hostile. Submariners were described at worst as pirates and spurned as being in a service that was 'no occupation for a gentleman'.

The four years of the First World War would change all that. Commodore Sidney Hall, the head of the Submarine service, was more than justified when he wrote in 1918, at the end of hostilities, that 'Your steadiness and grit, while the toll of your gallant fellows was heavy, have been beyond all praise and will form glorious pages in our naval history when this comes to be written.'

British submarines were deployed, in the main, in home waters, principally the North Sea, but it was in the Baltic and the Sea of Marmara that they found glory. In the Baltic they disrupted the vital iron ore trade and showed what well-handled submarines with determined commanding officers like Laurence and Horton could achieve. The submariners endured the rigours of the Russian winter and only ceased operations when Russia withdrew from the war after the Revolution.

The campaign in the Marmara confirmed the experience of the Baltic. After the hair-raising passage through the nets and minefields of the Dardanelles, the submarines played havoc with Turkish attempts to reinforce their armies on the Gallipoli Peninsula by sea and took the war right into the heart of the Turkish capital. Their efforts were not enough to prevent the British withdrawal, but they were a superb example of submarine warfare against an enemy supply line. Four of the five Victoria Crosses won by British submariners were awarded for operations in this theatre: to Lt N. D. Holbrook of *B11*, to Cdr E. C. Boyle of *E14*, to Lt Cdr M. Nasmith of *E11* and to Lt Cdr G. S. White of *E14*.

Generally, however, the lot of most British submarines was interminable patrols carried out in bad weather in heavily mined waters in the North Sea where targets were few. British submarines were the first naval units at sea in this theatre in 1914; and they were the last to return home in 1918.

The period also demonstrated considerable progress in submarine development, an astonishing variety of designs from British and overseas yards being evaluated by the Royal Navy. This ambitious experiment resulted in the Navy having more submarines than could be manned until order was restored by cancelling some and reallocating contracts for others. Some designs were less than successful, while others bordered on the fantastic. Nevertheless, the mood of experiment which dominated the infant Submarine Service produced some remarkable advances in submarine design and development. The 'R' Class for example, were years ahead of their time, while the steam-driven 'K' Class, though beset with mishaps and disasters, represented a considerable technical achievement unmatched by Germany or any of the Allies.

My sincere thanks are due to David Hill for producing the line drawings for this book and to Margaret Bidmead and Gus Britton of the Royal Navy Submarine Museum for their coffee and constructive criticism.

Paul Kemp

▲4 ▼5

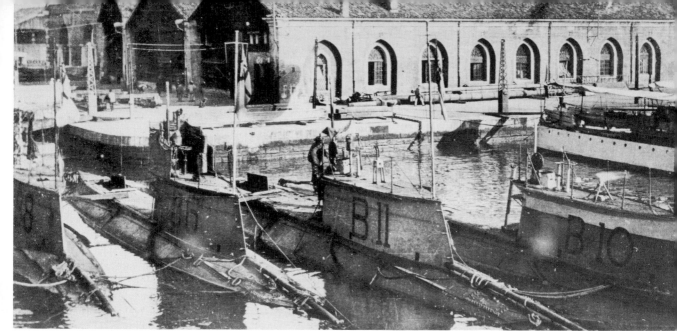

4. *B.1* the first of a class of eleven submarines which represented a considerable increase in size over the 'A' class. *B1*, *B3*, *B4* and *B5* spent the First World War in home waters (*B2* having been lost in collision in 1912), where they screened the movement of the BEF to France in August 1914. Their operational careers in home waters were brief, and by the end of 1916 none were on active service, having been either paid off or relegated to training or experimental duties.

5. It was in the Mediterranean that the old 'B' boats proved their worth – one to find glory and the other to find a different sort of fame. The photograph shows the crew of *B11*, with the commanding officer, Lt Norman Holbrook, after their epic voyage up the Dardanelles where they sank the 9,520-ton Turkish coast defence battleship *Messudieh* off Chanak on 13 December 1914 despite broaching after firing and becoming the target for every Turkish gun which would bear. When *B11* finally came out of the Narrows after a nine-hour dive, the air in the boat was so foul the petrol engine would not start. Holbrook received the Victoria Cross, his First Lieutenant the DSO and every member of the crew a DSM.

6. *B8*, *B6*, *B11* and *B10* at the Arsenal in Venice in 1916. In October 1915 the six 'B' boats in the Mediterranean were sent to Venice to assist the Italians in patrolling off the main Austrian base of Pola. They remained there for just over a year, carrying out 81 largely uneventful patrols. The only one to fire a torpedo was *B10*, which attacked, unsuccessfully, an Austrian merchant ship on 9 June 1916. *B11* scored the first success when, on 17 January 1916, she captured two Austrian airmen whose seaplane had been forced down with engine trouble.

7. *B.6* lying trimmed down on the surface while on patrol off Pola. Submarine tactics at the time were largely a matter of experiment, and with the primitive nature of the equipment available, it was considered that to spend the day dived might not be productive; accordingly, the submariners adopted a compromise – trimming the boat so that only the conning tower was above water. In the Adriatic, where Austrian air patrols were frequent and vigilant, this practice proved almost fatal on two occasions: *B9* on 30 March and *B7* on 4 June 1916 both endured a rough time at the hands of Austrian aircraft.

▲8

▲9 ▼10

8. *B10* in dry dock after sustaining severe damage during an Austrian air raid on Venice on the evening of 9 August 1916: the hole made by the bomb is visible on the port bow. She had just returned from patrol and secured alongside the depot ship *Marco Polo* when the siren sounded and everyone took cover. When the raid was over *B10* was found to have gone down – the first submarine to be sunk by aircraft. She was salved and placed in dock, but an Italian workman using cutting gear near one of her unemptied petrol tanks started a fire; in the ensuing panic the dock was flooded, which completed the submarine's destruction, and she was sold as scrap to the Italian government. Her sisters did not long survive her. They were withdrawn from Venice in October 1916 and converted to surface patrol craft for service on the Otranto Barrage. But their age told against them and they were paid off and scrapped soon after the war.

9. A group of 'C' Class submarines at Leith before the war. The 'Cs' were the first 'mass-production' British submarines, the Admiralty feeling that sufficient experience had been gained with the 'As' and 'Bs'. Yet the 'Cs' differed little from their predecessors: they still had petrol engines, internal ballast tanks and a single screw. The responsibility for failure to implement the lessons learned with the 'As' and 'Bs' lies with the Admiralty, who still saw the submarine as a weapon fit for little more than harbour defence. Despite their small size and lack of endurance, the 'Cs' saw continuous war service.

10. C27, which together with *C24* participated in one of the more unusual submarine operations of the First World War. In order to catch U-boats which were raiding the fishing fleets, it was decided to tow a 'C' Class submarine, submerged, behind a trawler, the two being linked together by a telephone line. If a U-boat was sighted the tow would be slipped and the submarine would, it was hoped,

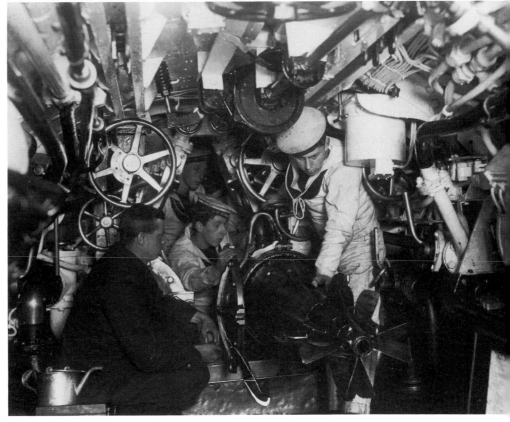

11▲ 12▼

torpedo the U-boat. Despite some technical hitches the idea worked: on 23 June 1915 *C24* under tow by the *Taranaki*, torpedoed *U40*, while on 20 July 1915 *C27*, towed by the *Princess Louise*, torpedoed *U23*.

11. *C29* was another of the 'Cs' involved in U-boat hunting with a trawler, but was not as lucky as her sisters. On 29 August 1915 she was proceeding, dived, in the tow of the trawler *Ariadne* off the Humber, in an area in which German submarines were very active. Those on board the *Ariadne* were horrified to see an explosion astern: *C29* had been towed into a mine. This marked the end of the trawler-submarine partnership.

12. A class under instruction in the fore ends of a 'C' Class submarine at Fort Blockhouse in 1918. The 18in torpedo was the armament for all British submarines of the First World War except the 'G', *H21*, *K26* and *L9* classes which were armed with the more powerful 21in weapon.

▲13

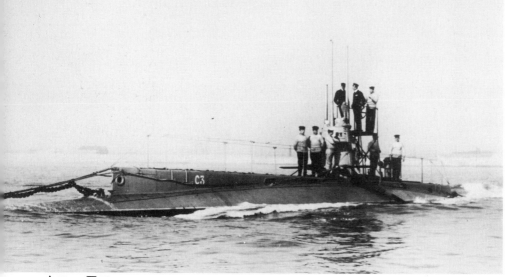

▲14 ▼15

13. *C32* mounted on a barge, leaving the floating dock at Archangel on 23 August 1916 to begin an unusual journey by river and canal to the Baltic. After the loss of *E13* the Admiralty decided against the sending of any more 'E' boats to the Baltic; instead, four 'C' boats, *C26*, *C27*, *C32* and *C35*, were towed to Archangel, mounted on barges and towed down to Kronstadt where they were prepared for short patrols in the Gulf of Riga. *C32* was destroyed to avoid capture on 22 October 1917 after grounding in Vaist Bay, Estonia.

14, 15. *C3* under way before the war. This submarine was selected for an apocalyptic end during the raid on Zeebrugge on 23 April 1918: packed with explosives, she was to be rammed into the viaduct connecting the Mole at Zeebrugge with the mainland, to prevent German reinforcements arriving while the main assault went ahead. Under the command of Lt Richard Sandford, *C3* was successfully placed in position, unmolested by the German guards who thought she was trying to pass under the viaduct. Sandford and his crew of five got away in a small skiff, despite three of them being wounded by rifle fire as they rowed away, and they were able to witness the five tons of explosives packed into *C3*'s fore ends blow an enormous hole in the viaduct. For this action Sandford was awarded the Victoria Cross, one of five VCs won by British submariners during the 1914–18 war.

16. German seaplanes strafing *C25* during her ordeal on 6 July 1918 off Harwich. The seaplanes were returning from a raid on Lowestoft and opened fire on *C25* with their machine-guns, killing the CO, Lt Bell, and fatally wounding the other three men on the bridge. Leading Seaman Barge, one of the wounded on the bridge, shouted to the First Lieutenant 'Dive, sir! Don't worry about me – I'm done for, anyway!' But the First Lieutenant struggled on to the bridge and dragged Barge down to the control room where he died as he was laid on the deck.

17. A view of *C25* as one of the German seaplanes flies overhead; the bridge is clear, so the photograph must have been taken after Barge had been dragged below. Inside the submarine the crew were trying plug the holes in the pressure hull made by the machine-gun bullets while the First Lieutenant prepared to dive the submarine, only to find that the lower conning tower hatch would not shut because the leg of one of the bodies on the bridge was jamming it. Two men were killed trying to free the hatch and eventually the First Lieutenant sawed the leg away. *C25* was eventually saved by the appearance of *E51* which drove off the aircraft. Leaking like a sieve and with her control room looking like an abattoir, *C25* was eventually towed back to Harwich.

18. *D1* goes down the ways at Barrow on 16 May 1908. She was launched without much ceremony and in conditions of some secrecy. The Admiralty's caution was justified for *D1* represented a considerable advance on the 'A', 'B' and 'C' Classes. She was the first British submarine to have saddle tanks, which gave greater space inside the hull; twin screws, which gave greater manoeuvrability; and diesel engines, which meant an end to the foul petrol fumes which had made life so unpleasant in the early boats. The 'D' Class were the Royal Navy's first submarines capable of extended operations overseas and were also fitted with W/T.

16▲

17▲   18▼

▲19

19. *D1* entering Portsmouth on completion, showing how her long, full-length casing and large conning tower made a clean break with the 'As', 'Bs' and 'Cs'. The capabilities of this new submarine were quickly shown by her young CO, Lt Noel Laurence, in the 1910

Manoeuvres when he 'torpedoed' two of 'Blue Fleet's cruisers. Another young CO, Lt Max Horton, in *D2*, penetrated the defences of the Firth of Forth to 'torpedo' his own depot ship. Both these officers were to make names for themselves in the 1914–18 war, in which three of

the eight 'D' boats would be sunk.

20. A 'D' Class submarine in dry dock, showing the arrangement of the two forward bow tubes with the bow 'cap', which served both tubes, in the 'open' position. Superimposing one

tube over another gave a finer shape to the bows but made the task of loading the torpedoes immensely more difficult. The photograph also shows the saddle tanks along the side of the hull.

▼20

21. *D5*, seen here leaving Portsmouth, was the first of the class to be lost when she was mined off Yarmouth on 3 November 1914. *D3*, *D5* and *E10* were lying off Gorleston when news was received of the German bombardment of Yarmouth and the three submarines were ordered to intercept the retiring German ships off Terschelling. Shortly after getting under way, *D5* was mined aft and sank quickly, leaving her CO, Lt Cdr Godfrey Herbert, and four others to be picked up by the trawler *Faithful*.

22. All the 'D' Class served in home waters during the First World War. *D4*, seen here before the war, had a narrow escape on 22 June 1915 when she tried to torpedo the German minelayer *Bielefeld* which had gone aground in the Heligoland Bight. Her CO, Lt Moncreiffe, decided to sink the escorting destroyer with a shallow-running torpedo and then surface to despatch the *Bielefeld*. However, the torpedo fired at the destroyer missed and *D4* found herself in shallow water being hunted by a destroyer. With 30ft showing on the depth gauge, Moncreiffe and his crew had to listen as the destroyer roared overhead, trying to ram the conning tower. Eventually the destroyer made off and Moncreiffe was able to surface and sink the *Bielefeld*.

23. *D7*'s bridge in 1918, showing the steel screen erected to give the bridge party protection from the elements; the boats generally had little more than a canvas screen, as shown in *D4* above. The damaged periscopes are the result of an encounter with a submerged German U-boat in May 1918. *D7* had already suffered from a case of 'mistaken identity': on 10 February 1918 she was depth-charged by the destroyer HMS *Pelican*, and the attack did considerable damage before *D7* was able to surface and establish her credentials.

21▲

22▲   23▼

▲24

▲25 ▼26

24. *E1* leaving Portsmouth. This boat was the first of class of 57 which bore the brunt of British submarine operations during the First World War. 'E' class boats served in every theatre of war and 29 were lost. *E1* was one of the first group of ten boats which were basically enlarged 'D' Class submarines in which the armament was rearranged to give single bow and stern tubes with two beam tubes firing port and starboard. She was also one of five 'E' boats to penetrate the Baltic, where she damaged the new German battlecruiser *Moltke* with a single torpedo on 19 August 1915. *E1* was eventually scuttled at Helsingfors on 3 April 1918 to prevent her falling into the hands of the advancing Germans.

25. *AE1* one of two of the first group of 'E' boats built for the Royal Australian Navy, was the first British submarine to be lost during the First World War. With her sister-boat *AE2* she had made the 83-day passage to Australia – no mean feat for such small craft. On the outbreak of war she participated in operations against the German colony at New Britain, and was last seen on 19 September off Blanche Bay by the destroyer *Parramatta*: she is believed to have struck a submerged reef. Her sister *AE2* was the first British submarine to enter the Sea of Marmara but was sunk on 30 April 1915 by the Turkish gunboat *Sultanhisar*.

26. *E4* at Harwich in the early days of the war. Her armament of four 6pdrs on high-angle mountings is certainly unusual and was a sign that the Zeppelins were making their presence felt. *E4* was commanded by Lt E. W. Leir, known as the 'Arch Thief' who plundered His Majesty's Navy of anything portable and about whom it was said that only his DSC was earned honestly. *E4* was eventually lost with all her crew in a collision with *E41* on 15 August 1916.

27. *E8* in wintry conditions in the Baltic, possibly at Reval. *E1*, *E8*, *E9*, *E18* and *E19* all made the dangerous journey to the Baltic, where they operated with the Russians. The submarines enjoyed some success against German shipping and endured considerable privations in the fierce Russian winters, during which they were icebound in harbour. *E18* was lost on 24 May 1916, the day after blowing the bows off the new destroyer *V100*; the remainder were blown up on 3–4 April 1918 to prevent their falling into the hands of the Bolsheviks.

28. Commander Max Horton (right) on the bridge of *E9* with his First Lieutenant, Lt Charles Chapman (left) and their Russian liaison officer (centre). Horton had already made a name for himself in the North Sea by sinking the German cruiser *Hela* on 13 September and the destroyer *S116* on 6 October 1914. His activities in the Baltic resulted in the virtual suspension of the iron ore trade from Sweden and caused the Germans to name the area 'Horton's Sea'.

29. *E13* stranded off the Danish island of Salthome on 18 August 1915. The boat had been ordered into the Baltic but had run aground because of a defective gyro-compass. Her CO, Lt G. Layton, was warned by the Danes that he had twenty-four hours to refloat the submarine or else be interned under international law. A German torpedo-boat, *G132*, was also standing by, observing proceedings but making no attempt to interfere.

▲ 29

30. *E13* in the harbour at Copenhagen and showing the scars of indiscriminate German shellfire. Although the torpedo-boat *G132* respected Danish neutrality, she was replaced by two other destroyers which promptly began to shell and machine-gun the stranded submarine. Fourteen members of *E13*'s crew were killed or were

▼ 30

to die of their wounds, and many more would have been killed were it not for the Danish torpedo-boat *Soulven*, which placed herself between the submarine and her assailants. *E13* was eventually sold for scrap in Denmark in December 1921.

31. *E14* at Mudros, about to sail for her first patrol in the Sea of Marmara. Commanded by Lt Cdr E. C. Boyle, she was the second British submarine to enter the Marmara but was the first to return. *E15* had been sunk on 17 April 1915 while attempting to penetrate the Narrows, and *AE2*, which managed to enter the Marmara was sunk by the Turkish gunboat *Sultanhisar* on 30 April 1915. Boyle spent 22

days in the Marmara and on his return was awarded the Victoria Cross. *E14* spent the rest of the war in the Mediterranean and was eventually lost on 28 January 1918 while trying to penetrate the Dardanelles to torpedo the stranded *Goeben*; her CO, Lt Cdr G. S. White, was posthumously awarded the VC.

32. *E11* (Lt M. Nasmith) returns to Mudros on 7 June to the cheers of the Fleet, having completed the second British submarine patrol in the Sea of Marmara, for which he too was awarded the VC. Nasmith sank a gunboat and six merchant ships, and forced another merchant ship to beach herself. On 25 May 1915 Nasmith took the war into the heart of the Turkish Empire when he entered Constantinople harbour in search of the *Goeben* and *Breslau*. He found neither, but he torpedoed the steamer, *Istanbul* lying at the Topkhana Arsenal and then had to avoid one of his own torpedoes which ran wild and threatened to sink a neutral American cruiser.

34▶

▲33

35▼

33, 34. *E11*'s crew pose on the casing after their return to Mudros. Damage to one of their periscopes can be clearly seen. This was sustained on 23 May when *E11* encountered the Turkish gunboat *Peleng I Derya*, which was swiftly despatched with a torpedo. However, the Turks continued to fire on the periscopes, taking a neat piece out of one of them (as shown in the inset), and for the rest of the patrol Nasmith had to operate with only one periscope. *E11*'s second patrol lasted from 5 August to 2 September and was crowned by the sinking of the Turkish battleship *Heireddin Barbarossa* on 8 August.

35. *E2* returns to Mudros after a fraught patrol in the Marmara from 13 August to 14 September. She operated with *E11* with some success and also attempted to cut the Constantinople–Adrianople railway line by sending the First Lieutenant, Lt L. V. Lyon, ashore with a demolition charge. Although a loud explosion was heard, nothing more was ever seen of Lyon.

36. Lt Cdr E. de B. Stocks standing by *E2*'s collapsed 12pdr mounting after his return to Mudros. The mounting had been badly strained during the passage up the Narrows, having become entangled in some of the nets, and some two days' hard work was required before the gun was serviceable. Then, in an action

with *E11* against a Turkish 'Q' ship the mounting collapsed, but *E2*'s hard-pressed engineering department once again effected temporary repairs that enabled the submarine, with *E11*, to carry out a very successful bombardment at Mudania.

37. *E7* (Lt Cdr A. D. Cochrane) sails from Mudros for her second and last patrol in the Sea of

Marmara. While proceeding up the Narrows by Nagara Point she became entangled with the submarine net and could not get free. Cochrane's efforts to free *E7* had not gone unobserved, and the submarine was located and blown to the surface with mines lowered from a rowing boat manned by *Oberleutnant* Heino von Heimburg, commanding

officer of a German U-boat under repair at Chanak, and his cook! Cochrane and his ship's company became prisoners-of-war but in August 1918 Cochrane escaped and succeeded in reaching Cyprus.

36▲

37▼

▲38

38. The crew of *E20* pose proudly with their new submarine at Barrow in 1915. *E20* went straight to the Dardanelles from the UK, where it was hoped she could use the 6in howitzer, just visible on the casing, to good effect against Turkish troops and shipping. She successfully negotiated the Narrows but her rendezvous position with the French submarine *Turquoise* was compromised when documents were found after the latter had been abandoned. Instead of the *Turquoise*, *E20* met the German *UB14*, which sank her with a single torpedo on 6 November 1915.

▼39

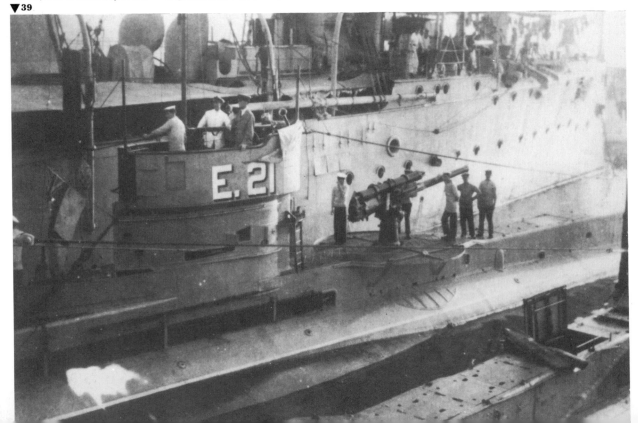

39. *E21* alongside the Italian depot ship *Lombardia* at Brindisi in 1918. When the Dardanelles campaign finished the 'E' boats were redeployed to the Adriatic and eventually *E2*, *E11*, *E12*, *E21*, *E25*, *E46* and *E48* served there. Their time in the Adriatic was singularly unsuccessful, *E21* being the only British submarine to sink an Austrian merchant ship, the 405grt *Vila* on 30 June 1918. One of her more merciful failures was when she mistakenly attacked the Austrian hospital ship *Baron Call* loaded with 855 wounded: one torpedo struck but failed to explode.

40. *E22* with two Sopwith Schneider seaplanes on her after casing. The seaplanes were intended for bombing Zeppelin bases and shooting down Zeppelins approaching the English coast. This was the Royal Navy's first experiment at carrying aircraft on a submarine. To launch the seaplane the submarine trimmed down and the seaplane floated off to take off under its own power. Recovery was equally simple: the seaplane landed alongside the submarine and was assisted back on to the casing while the submarine lay trimmed down. It was an ingenious scheme but impractical. The seaplanes could only be launched in very calm weather and the submarine could not dive without jettisoning them. *E22* never used her Sopwiths operationally and she herself was torpedoed in the North Sea by the German *UB18* on 25 April 1916.

41. The launch of *E27* at Yarrow's Scotstoun yard on 9 June 1917; the photograph clearly shows the saddle-tank design of the hull. The 'E' class marked the end of a logical progression of British submarine development from *A1*. Under the twin stimuli of the 1912 Submarine Committee and inaccurate intelligence assessments of the capabilities of foreign submarines, particularly German U-boats, the Admiralty began investigating a variety of different hull forms and means of propulsion, and it would not be until the advent of the 'L' Class that the saddle-tank hull-form returned to the Royal Navy.

'A' CLASS

Displacement: 190 tons surfaced, 205–207 tons dived.

Dimensions: (A1) 31.5m × 3.6m × 3.1m; (A2–A13) 32m × 3.9m × 3.3m.

Machinery: (A1–A12) One shaft, 16-cylinder Wolseley petrol engine, one electric motor, 350hp/125hp for 9½/6 knots; (A2–A4) 450hp/150hp for 10/7 knots; (A5–A7) 550hp/150hp for 11½/7 knots; (A8–A12) 600hp/150hp for 11/6 knots; (A13) one shaft, 6-cylinder heavy oil engine, one electric motor, 500hp/150hp for 11/6 knots. Endurance 320nm at 10 knots surfaced.

Armament: (A1–A4) One 18in bow torpedo tube, 3 torpedoes; (A5–A13) two 18in bow torpedo tubes, 4 torpedoes.

Complement: 11 officers and men.

A1 (ordered as *Holland 6*, launched Vickers 9.7.02, sunk as target 8.11); A2 (Vickers 16.4.04, wrecked 1920 while awaiting disposal; A3 (Vickers 9.3.03, sunk as target 17.5.12); A4 (Vickers 9.6.03, sold for BU 16.1.20); A5 (Vickers 3.3.04 sold for BU 1920); A6 (Vickers 3.3.04, sold for BU 16.1.20); A7 (Vickers 23.1.05, lost in Whitesand Bay 16.1.14); A8 (Vickers 23.1.05, sold 8.10.20); A9 (Vickers 8.2.05, sold for BU 1920); A10 (Vickers 8.2.05, sold for BU 1.4.19); A11 (Vickers 8.3.05, sold for BU 5.20); A12 (Vickers 8.3.05, sold for BU 16.1.20); A13 (Vickers 18.4.05, sold for BU 1920).

'B' CLASS

Displacement: 287 tons surfaced, 316 tons dived.

Dimensions: 43.3m × 4.1m × 3.4m.

Machinery: One shaft, 16-cylinder Vickers petrol engine, one electric motor, 600hp/290hp for 12/6 knots. Endurance 1,000nm at 8¾ knots.

Armament: Two 18in bow torpedo tubes, 4 torpedoes.

Complement: 15 officers and men.

All built by Vickers. B1 (25.10.04, sold for BU May 1921); B2 (30.10.05, sunk in collision with SS *Amerika* in Dover Strait 4.10.12); B3 (31.10.05, sold for BU 12.19); B4 (14.11.05, sold for BU 4.19); B5 (14.11.05, sold for BU 8.21); B6 (30.11.05, sold for BU 1919); B7 (30.11.05, sold for BU 1919); B8 (23.1.06, sold for BU 1919); B9 (24.1.06, sold for BU 1919); B10 (23.3.06, war loss 9.8.16); B11 (21.2.06, sold for BU 1919).

'C' CLASS

Displacement: 287–290 tons surfaced, 316–320 tons dived.

Dimensions: 43.3m × 4.1m × 3.4–3.5m.

Machinery: One shaft, 16-cylinder Vickers petrol engine, one electric motor, 600hp/300hp for 13/7½ knots. Endurance 1,000nm at 8 knots surfaced.

Armament: Two 18in bow torpedo tubes, 4 torpedoes.

Complement: 16 officers and men.

All built by Vickers except for C17–C20, C33 and C34 (Chatham: the first submarines to be built by a Royal Dockyard). C1 (10.7.06, sold for BU 10.20); C2 (10.7.06, sold for BU 10.20); C3 (3.10.06, expended during Zeebrugge Raid 23.4.18); C4 (18.10.06, sold for BU 4.22); C5 (20.8.06, sold for BU 10.19); C6 (20.8.06, sold for BU 11.19); C7 (15.2.07, sold for BU 12.19); C8 (15.2.07, sold for BU 10.20); C9 (3.4.07, sold for BU 7.22); C10 (15.4.07, sold for BU 7.22); C11 (27.5.07, sunk in collision with SS *Eddystone* off Cromer 14.7.09); C12 (9.9.07, sold for BU 2.20); C13 (9.11.07, sold for BU 2.20); C14 (7.12.07), sold for BU 12.21); C15 (21.1.08, sold for BU 2.22); C16 (19.3.08, sold for BU 8.22); C17 (13.3.08, sold for BU 11.19); C18 (10.10.08, sold for BU 5.21); C19 (20.3.09, sold for BU 2.20); C20 (27.11.09, sold for BU 5.21); C21 26.9.08, sold for BU 12.21); C22 (10.10.08, sold for BU 2.20); C23 (26.11.08, sold for BU 12.21); C24 (26.11.08, sold for BU 5.21); C25 (10.3.09, sold for BU 12.21); C26 (20.3.09, scuttled in Baltic 4.4.18); C27 (22.4.09, scuttled in Baltic 5.4.18); C28 (22.4.09, sold for BU 8.21); C29 (19.6.09, war loss 29.8.15); C30 (19.7.09, sold for BU 8.21); C31 (2.9.09, war loss on or around 4.1.15); C32 (29.9.09, stranded 22.10.17 and abandoned); C33 (2.11.09, scuttled in Baltic 4.4.18); C34 (8.6.10, war loss 17.7.17); C35 (2.11.09, scuttled in Baltic 5.4.18); C36 (30.11.09, sold for BU 6.19); C37 (1.1.10, sold for BU 6.19); C38 (10.2.10, sold for BU 6.19).

'D' CLASS

Displacement: (D1) 483 tons surfaced, 595 tons dived; (D2) 489 tons surfaced, 603 tons dived; (D3–D8) 495 tons surfaced, 620 tons dived.

Dimensions: (D1) 49.7m × 6.2m × 3.2m; (D2) 49.4m × 6.3m over tanks × 3.3m; (D3–D8) 50.2m × 6.2m over tanks × 3.5m.

Machinery: Two shafts, 6-cylinder diesels, two electric motors, 1,200hp/550hp for 14/9 knots. Endurance 2,500nm at 10 knots surfaced.

Armament: Three 18in torpedo tubes (two bow, one stern), 6 torpedoes; one 12pdr (D4 76mm) gun fitted later.

Complement: 25 officers and men.

All built by Vickers except D7 and D8 (Chatham Dockyard). D1 (16.5.08, sunk as a target 23.10.18); D2 (25.5.10, war loss 25.11.14); D3 (17.10.10, war loss 15.3.18); D4 (27.5.11, sold for BU 12.21); D5 (28.8.11, war loss 3.11.14); D6 (23.10.11, war loss 26.6.18); D7 (14.1.11, sold for BU 2.21); D8 (23.9.11, sold for BU 12.21).

'E' CLASS (*E1* GROUP)

Displacement: 655 tons surfaced, 796 tons dived.

Dimensions: 54.2m × 6.9m × 3.8m.

Machinery: Two shafts, 8-cylinder Vickers diesels, 2 electric motors, 1,600hp/840hp for 15 knots/9 knots. Endurance 3,000nm at 10 knots surfaced.

Armament: Four 18in torpedo tubes (one bow, two beam, one stern), 8 torpedoes; one 12pdr gun.

Complement: 30 officers and men.

E1 (ex-D9, Chatham DY 9.11.12, scuttled in Baltic 3.4.18); E2 (ex-D10, Chatham DY 23.11.12, sold for BU 7.3.21); E3 (Vickers 29.10.12, war loss 18.10.14); E4 (Vickers 5.2.12, sold for BU 21.2.22); E5 (Vickers 17.5.12, war loss 7.3.16); E6 (Vickers 12.11.12, war loss 26.12.16); E7 (Chatham DY 2.10.13, war loss 4.9.15); E8 (Chatham DY 30.10.13, scuttled in Baltic 3.4.18); AE1 (Vickers 22.5.13, lost by unknown cause off Bismarck Archipelago 19.9.14); AE2 (Vickers 18.6.13, war loss 30.4.15).

'E' CLASS (*E9* GROUP)

Displacement: 667 tons surfaced, 807 tons dived.

Dimensions: 55.2m (from *E19* on, 55.6m) × 4.6m × 3.8m.

Machinery: As *E1* group.

Armament: Five 18in torpedo tubes (two bow, one stern, two beam), 10 torpedoes; one 12pdr gun. E24, E34, E41, E45, E46 and E51 carried no beam tubes

but 20 mines in ten vertical wells in saddle tanks.
Complement: 30 officers and men.
E9 (Vickers 29.11.13, scuttled in Baltic 18.4.18); *E10* (Vickers 29.11.13, war loss 18.1.15); *E11* (Vickers 23.4.14, sold for BU 7.3.21); *E12* (Chatham DY 5.9.14, sold for BU 7.3.21); *E13* (Chatham DY 22.9.14, war loss 3.9.15); *E14* (Vickers 7.7.14, war loss 27.1.18); *E15* (Vickers 23.4.14, war loss 17.4.15); *E16* (Vickers 23.9.14, war loss 22.8.16); *E17* (Vickers 16.1.15, wrecked off Texel 6.1.16); *E18* (Vickers 4.3.15, war loss 24.5.16); *E19* (Vickers 13.5.15, scuttled in Baltic 3.4.18); *E20* (Vickers 12.6.15, war loss 5.11.15); *E21* (Vickers 24.7.15, sold for BU 14.12.21); *E22* (27.8.15, war loss 24.5.16); *E23* (Vickers 28.9.15, sold for BU 6.9.22); *E24* (Vickers 9.12.15, war loss 24.3.16); *E25* (Beardmore 23.8.15, sold for BU 14.12.21); *E26* (Beardmore 11.11.15, war loss 6.7.16); *E27* (Yarrow 9.6.17, sold for BU 6.9.22); *E28* (Yarrow, cancelled 20.4.15); *E29* (Armstrong 1.6.15, sold for BU 1.2.22); *E30* (Armstrong 29.6.15, war loss 22.11.16); *E31* (Scotts 23.8.15, sold for BU 9.22); *E32* (White 16.8.16, sold for BU 6.9.22); *E33* (Thornycroft 18.4.16, sold for BU 9.22); *E34* (Thornycroft 27.1.17, war loss 20.7.18); *E35* (J. Brown 20.5.16, sold for BU 6.9.22); *E36* (J. Brown 16.9.16, war loss 17.1.17); *E37* (Fairfield 2.9.15, war loss 1.12.16); *E38* (Fairfield 13.6.15, sold for BU 6.9.22); *E39* (Palmer 18.5.16, sold for BU 13.10.21, foundered in tow 9.22); *E40* (Palmer 9.11.16, sold for BU 14.12.21); *E41* (Cammell Laird 28.7.15, sold for BU 6.9.22); *E42* (Cammell Laird 22.10.15, sold for BU 6.9.22); *E43* (Swan Hunter 1916, sold for BU 3.1.21); *E44* (Swan Hunter 21.2.16, sold for BU 13.10.21); *E45* (Cammell Laird 2.5.16, sold for BU 6.9.22); *E46* (Cammell Laird 4.4.16, sold for BU 6.9.22); *E47* (Fairfield 29.5.16, war loss 20.8.17); *E48* (Fairfield 2.8.16, sold for BU 7.28); *E49* (Swan Hunter 18.9.16, war loss 12.3.17); *E50* (J. Brown 3.11.16, war loss 1.2.18); *E51* (Yarrow [transferred Scotts 3.15] 30.11.16, sold for BU 3.10.21; *E52* (Yarrow [transferred Denny 3.15] 25.1.17, sold for BU 3.1.21); *E53* (Beardmore 1916, sold for BU 6.9.22); *E54* (Beardmore 1916, sold for BU 14.2.21); *E55* (Denny 5.2.16, sold for BU 6.9.22); *E56* (Denny 19.6.16, sold for BU 19.6.23); *E57* (see *L1*); *E5* (see *L2*).

NAUTILUS

Displacement: 1,441 tons surfaced, 2,026 tons dived.
Dimensions: 78.8m × 7.9m × 5.4m.
Machinery: Two shafts, Vickers 12-cylinder diesels, two electric motors, 3,700hp/1,000hp for 17/10 knots. Endurance 5,300nm at 11 knots.
Armament: Eight 18in torpedo tubes (2 bow, 4 beam, 2 stern), 16 torpedoes; one 3in AA gun.
Complement: 42 officers and men.
Built by Vickers 31.12.14, sold for BU 6.22.

SWORDFISH

Displacement: 932 tons surfaced, 1,105 tons dived.
Dimensions: 70.5m × 7m × 4.5m.
Machinery: Two shafts, Parsons geared impulse-reaction steam turbines, one Yarrow boiler, two electric motors, 4,000hp/1,400hp for 18/10 knots. Endurance 3,000nm at 8.5 knots surfaced.
Armament: Two 21in bow torpedo tubes, 2 torpedoes; four 18in beam torpedo tubes, 8 torpedoes; two 3in guns.
Complement: About 18 officers and men.
Built by Scotts 18.3.16, sold for BU 7.22.

'G' CLASS

Displacement: 703 tons surfaced, 837 tons submerged.
Dimensions: 57m × 6.9m × 4.1m.
Machinery: Two shafts, Vickers 8-cylinder diesels, two electric motors, 1,600hp/840hp for 14.5 knots/9 knots. Endurance 2,400nm at 12.5 knots surfaced.
Armament: One 21in stern torpedo tube, 2 torpedoes; four 18in torpedo tubes (2 bow, 2 beam), 8 torpedoes.
Complement: 30 officers and men.
G1 (Chatham DY 14.8.15, sold for BU 14.2.20); *G2* (Chatham DY 23.12.15, sold for BU 16.1.20); *G3* (Chatham DY 22.1.16, sold for BU 4.11.21); *G4* (Chatham DY 23.10.15, sold for BU 27.6.28); *G5* (Chatham Dockyard 23.11.15, sold for BU 25.10.22); *G6* (Armstrong 7.12.15, sold 4.11.21); *G7* (Armstrong 4.3.16, war loss 1.11.18); *G8* (Vickers 1.5.16, war loss 14.1.18); *G9* (Vickers 15.6.16, war loss 16.9.17); *G10* (Vickers 11.1.16, sold for BU 20.1.23); *G11* (Vickers 22.2.16, wrecked off Hawick 22.11.18); *G12* (24.3.16, sold for BU 14.2.20); *G13* (Vickers 18.7.16, sold for BU 20.1.23); *G14* (Scotts 17.5.17, sold for BU 11.3.21); *G15*

(ordered J. S. White 30.9.14, cancelled 20.4.15).

'J' CLASS

Displacement: 1,204 tons surfaced, 1,820 tons dived (*J7* 1,212/1,820 tons).
Dimensions: 84m (*J7* 83.7m) × 7m × 4.3m.
Machinery: Three shafts, Vickers 12-cylinder diesels, three electric motors, 3,600hp/1,350hp for 19.5 knots/9.5 knots. Endurance 5,000nm at 12.5 knots surfaced.
Armament: Six 18in torpedo tubes (four bow, two beam), 12 torpedoes; one 12pdr gun, one 3in AA gun (*J5–J7* one 12pdr AA, one 2pdr). All except *J3* later rearmed with one 4in. *J1* fitted with depth-charge chutes.
Complement: 44 officers and men.
J1 (Portsmouth DY 11.15, to RAN 1919, scuttled 26.5.26); *J2* (Portsmouth DY 11.15, to RAN 1919, scuttled 1.26); *J3* (Pembroke DY, cancelled 20.4.15); *J3* (ex-*J7*, renamed 4.15, Pembroke DY 4.12.15, to RAN 1919, sold for BU 1.26); *J4* (Pembroke DY, cancelled 20.4.15); *J4* (ex-*J8*, renamed 4.15, Pembroke DY 2.2.16, to RAN 1919, sold as *J1* but sank at moorings 10.7.24, raised and scuttled 1927); *J5* (Devonport DY 9.9.15, to RAN 1919, scuttled 4.6.26); *J6* (Devonport DY 9.9.15, war loss 15.10.18); *J7* (Devonport DY 21.2.17, to RAN 1919, sold for BU 11.29).

'K' CLASS

Displacement: 1,980 tons surfaced, 2,566 tons dived.
Dimensions: 100.6m × 8.1m × 5.2m.
Machinery: Two shafts, Brown Curtis (*K3, K4, K8–10, K17* Parsons) geared steam turbines, two Yarrow boilers, four electric motors, 10,500hp/1,440hp for 24/9.5 knots. Endurance 3,000nm at 13.5 knots surfaced.
Armament: Ten 18in torpedo tubes (four bow, four beam, one twin revolving mount in casing); two 4in QF guns, one 3in AA gun.
Complement: 59 officers and men.
K1 (Portsmouth DY 14.11.16, sunk after collision with *K4* 17.11.17); *K2* (Portsmouth DY 14.10.16, sold for BU 13.7.26); *K3* (Vickers 20.5.16, sold for BU 26.10.21); *K4* (Vickers 15.7.16, sunk following collision with *K6* 31.1.18); *K5* (Portsmouth DY 16.12.16, sunk in Bay of Biscay 20.1.21); *K6* (Devonport DY 31.5.16, sold for BU 13.7.26); *K7*

(Devonport DY 31.5.16, sold for BU 9.9.21); *K8* (Vickers 10.10.16, sold for BU 11.10.23); *K9* (Vickers 8.11.16, sold for BU 23.7.26); *K10* (Vickers 27.12.16, sold for BU 4.11.21 but foundered in tow 10.1.22); *K11* (Armstrong 16.8.16, sold for BU 4.11.21); *K12* (Armstrong 23.2.17, sold for BU 23.7.26); *K13* (Fairfield 11.11.16, foundered on trials 29.1.17, salved and renumbered *K22*, sold for BU 16.12.26); *K14* (Fairfield 8.2.17, sold for BU 1926); *K15* (Scots 30.10.17, sold for BU 8.24); *K16* (Beardmore 5.11.17, sold 22.8.24); *K17* (Vickers 10.4.17, sunk in collision with HMS *Fearless* 21.1.18); *K18* (see *M1*); *K19* (see *M2*); *K20* (see *M3*); *K21* (see *M4*).

MODIFIED 'K' CLASS

Displacement: 2,140 tons surfaced, 2,530 tons dived.
Dimensions: 107m × 8.5m × 4.9m
Machinery: Two shafts, Parsons geared turbines, two Yarrow boilers, four electric motors, 10,500hp/1,440hp for 23.5/9.5 knots.
Armament: Six 21in bow torpedo tubes, 12 torpedoes; four 18in beam torpedo tubes, 8 torpedoes; three 4in QF guns.
Complement: 59 officers and men.
K23 (Armstrong, cancelled 1919); *K24* (Armstrong, cancelled 1919); *K25* (Armstrong, cancelled 1919); *K26* (Vickers 26.8.19, sold for BU 3.31); *K27* (Vickers, cancelled 1919); *K28* (Vickers, cancelled 1919).

'M' CLASS

Displacement: 1,594 tons surfaced, 1,946 tons dived.
Dimensions: 90.1m × 7.5m × 4.9m.
Machinery: Two shafts, Vickers 12-cylinder diesels, two electric motors, 1,499hp/1,600hp for 15/9 knots. Endurance 3,840nm at 10 knots surfaced.
Armament: Four 18in bow torpedo tubes; one 12in BL 30-cal. Mk IX gun; one 3in AA gun.
Complement: 65 officers and men.
M1 (ex-*K18*, renamed 1917, Vickers 9.7.17, rammed and sunk in collision with SS *Vidar* off Start Point 12.11.25); *M2* (ex-*K19*, renamed 1917, Vickers 19.10.18, converted to carry seaplane at Chatham 4.28, sunk off Portland

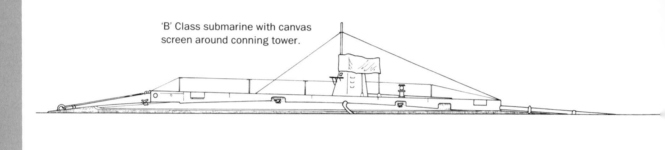

'B' Class submarine with canvas screen around conning tower.

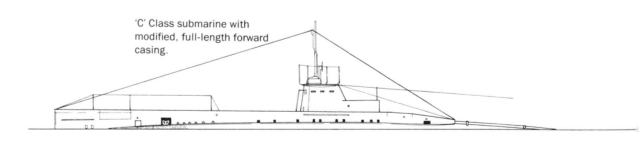

'C' Class submarine with modified, full-length forward casing.

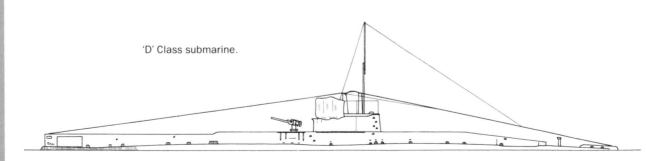

'D' Class submarine.

26.1.32); M3 (ex-*K20*, renamed 1917, Armstrong 19.10.20, converted to mine-layer 1927, sold for BU 2.32); M4 (ex-*K21*, renamed 1917, Armstrong, cancelled and hull launched to clear slip, sold for BU 30.11.21).

'S' CLASS

Displacement: 265 tons surfaced, 324 tons dived.
Dimensions: 45.1m × 4.4m × 3.2m.
Machinery: Two shafts, Scott-Fiat 6-cylinder diesels, two electric motors, 650hp/400hp for 13/8.5 knots. Endurance 1,600nm at 8.5 knots surfaced.
Armament: Two 18in bow torpedo tubes, 4 torpedoes; one 12pdr gun.
Complement: 18 officers and men.

All built by Scotts. S1 (28.2.14); S2 (14.4.15); S3 (10.6.15). All transferred to Royal Italian Navy 25.10.15.

'V' CLASS

Displacement: (V1) 386 tons surfaced, 453 tons dived; (V2–V4) 391 tons surfaced, 457 tons dived.
Dimensions: (V1) 43.9m × 5m × 3.5m; (V2–V4) 45m × 5m × 3.5m.
Machinery: Two shafts, 8-cylinder Vickers diesels, two electric motors, 900hp/450hp for 14/8.5 knots. Endurance 3,000nm at 9 knots surfaced.
Armament: Two 18in bow torpedo tubes, 4 torpedoes; one 12pdr gun.
Complement: 20 officers and men.
All built by Vickers.

V1 (23.7.14, sold for BU 11.21); V2 (17.2.15, sold for BU 11.21); V3 (1.4.15, sold for BU 10.20); V4 25.11.15, sold for BU 10.20).

'W' CLASS

Displacement: (W1, W2) 331 tons surfaced, 449 tons dived; (W3, W4) 321 tons surfaced, 479 tons dived.
Dimensions: (W1, W2) 52.4m × 4.7m × 2.7m; (W3, W4) 45.7m × 5.4m × 2.8m.
Machinery: (W1, W2) Two shafts, 8-cylinder diesels, two electric motors, 710hp/480hp for 13/8.5 knots. Endurance 2,500nm at 9 knots surfaced. (W3, W4) Two shafts, 6-cylinder diesels, two electric motors, 760hp/480hp for 13/8.5 knots.

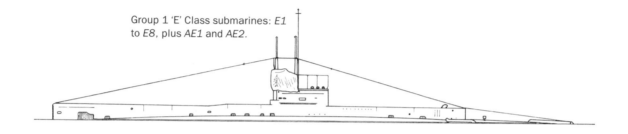

Group 1 'E' Class submarines: E1 to E8, plus *AE1* and *AE2*.

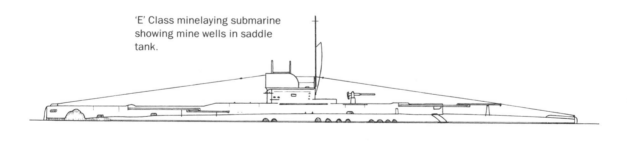

'E' Class minelaying submarine showing mine wells in saddle tank.

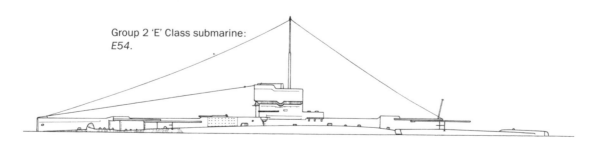

Group 2 'E' Class submarine: *E54*.

Armament: (*W1*, *W2*) Two 18in bow torpedo tubes, 2 torpedoes; four 18in torpedoes in external drop collars. (*W3*, *W4*) Two 18in bow torpedo tubes, 4 torpedoes. One 3in AA gun added in both.
Complement: 18 officers and men.
All built by Armstrong. *W1* (19.11.14); *W2* (15.2.15); *W3* (1.4.15); *W4* (25.11.15). All transferred to Royal Italian Navy in August 1916.

'F' CLASS

Displacement: 363 tons surfaced, 525 tons dived.
Dimensions: 46m × 4.9m × 3.2m.
Machinery: Two shafts, 2 Vickers (*F2* MAN) diesels, 2 electric motors, 900hp/ 400hp for 14/8.75 knots. Endurance

3,000nm at 9.5 knots surfaced.
Armament: Three 18in torpedo tubes (two bow, one stern), 6 torpedoes; one 2pdr gun.
Complement: 19 officers and men.
F1 (Chatham DY 31.3.15, sold for BU 1920); *F2* (J. S. White 7.7.17, sold for BU 7.22); *F3* (Thornycroft 19.2.16, sold for BU 1920).

'H' CLASS

Displacement: 364 tons surfaced, 434 tons dived.
Dimensions: 45.8m × 4.7m × 3.8m.
Machinery: Two shafts, diesels, 2 electric motors, 480hp/620hp for 13/11 knots. Endurance 1,600nm at 10 knots surfaced.

Armament: Four 18in bow torpedo tubes, 8 torpedoes.
Complement: 22 officers and men.
NB: Dates given for 'H' Class are dates of completion not launch.
H1 (Vickers Montreal 5.15, sold for BU 7.3.21); *H2* (Vickers Montreal 5.15, sold for BU 7.3.21); *H3* (Vickers Montreal 3.6.15, war loss 15.7.16); *H4* (Vickers Montreal 3.6.15, sold for BU 30.11.21); *H5* (Vickers Montreal 21.6.15, sunk in collision in Irish Sea 6.3.18); *H6* (Vickers Montreal 10.6.15, stranded on Dutch Coast 18.1.16, interned and sold to Dutch Navy as *O8* 1919); *H7* (Vickers Montreal 20.6.15, sold for BU 30.11.21); *H8* (Vickers Montreal 18.5.15, sold for BU 29.11.21); *H9* (Vickers Montreal 15.6.15, sold for BU

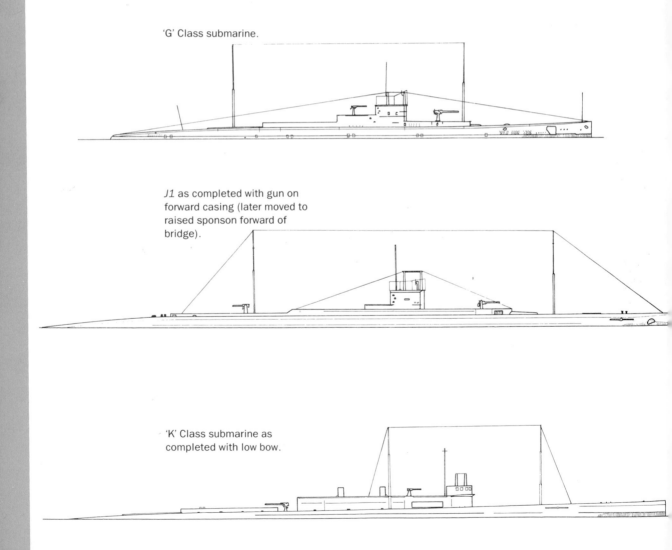

'G' Class submarine.

J1 as completed with gun on forward casing (later moved to raised sponson forward of bridge).

'K' Class submarine as completed with low bow.

30.11.21); *H10* (Vickers Montreal 27.6.15, war loss 19.1.18); *H11* (Fore River Shipbuilding Co. sold for BU 1921); *H12* (Fore River Shipbuilding Co. 1915, sold for BU 4.22); *H13* (Fore River Shipbuilding Co. 3.7.17, completed for Chilean Navy as *Gualcolda*); *H14* (Fore River Shipbuilding Co. 1918, to RCN as *CH14*, sold for BU 1925); *H15* (Fore River Shipbuilding Co. 1918, to RCN, as *CH15*, sold for BU 1925); *H16* (Fore River Shipbuilding Co. 3.7.1917, completed for Chilean Navy as *Teguada*); *H17* (Fore River Shipbuilding Co. 1917, completed for Chilean Navy as *Rucumilla*); *H18* (Fore River Shipbuilding Co. 7.17, completed for Chilean Navy as *Guale*); *H19* (Fore River Shipbuilding Co. 7.17, completed for Chilean Navy as *Quidora*); *H20*

(Fore River Shipbuilding Co. 7.17, completed for Chilean Navy as *Fresia*).

MODIFIED 'H' CLASS

Displacement: 423 tons surfaced, 510 tons dived.
Dimensions: 52.4m × 4.8m × 4m.
Machinery: Two shafts, diesels, 2 electric motors, 480hp/620hp for 11.5/10.5 knots.
Armament: Four 21in bow torpedo tubes, 6/8 torpedoes.
Complement: 22 officers and men.
H21 (Vickers 20.10.17, sold for BU 13.7.26); *H22* (Vickers 14.11.17, sold for BU 19.2.29); *H23* (Vickers 29.1.18, sold for BU 4.5.34); *H24* (Vickers 14.11.17, sold for BU 4.5.34); *H25*

(Vickers 27.4.18, sold for BU 19.2.29); *H26* (Vickers 15.11.17, sold for BU 21.4.28); *H27* (Vickers 25.9.18, sold for BU 30.8.35); *H28* (Vickers 12.3.18, sold for BU 18.8.34); *H29* (Vickers 8.6.18, sold for BU 7.10.27); *H30* (Vickers 9.5.18, sold for BU 30.8.35); *H31* (Vickers 19.11.18, sunk in Bay of Biscay 24.12.41); *H32* (Vickers 19.11.18, sold for BU 18.10.44); *H33* (Cammell Laird 24.8.18, sold for BU 1944); *H34* (Cammell Laird 5.11.18, sold for BU 1945); *H35* (Cammell Laird, cancelled 1919); *H36* (Cammell Laird, cancelled 1919); *H37* (Cammell Laird, cancelled 1919); *H38* (Cammell Laird, cancelled 1919); *H39* (Cammell Laird, cancelled 1919); *H40* (Cammell Laird, cancelled 1919); *H41* (Armstrong 1918, damaged in col-

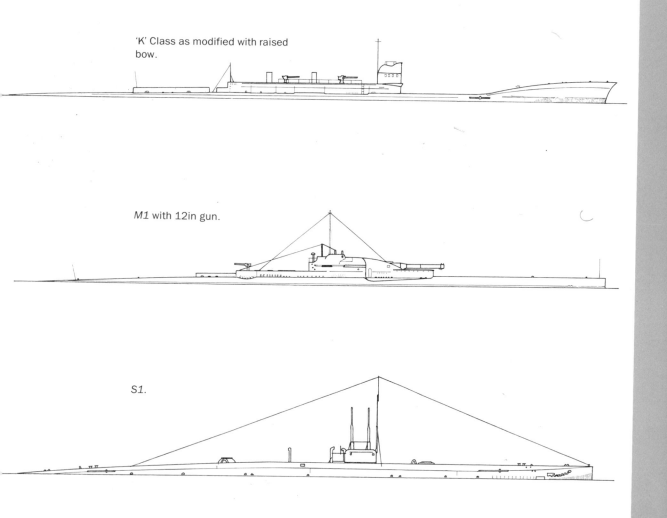

'K' Class as modified with raised bow.

M1 with 12in gun.

S1.

lision 1920, sold for BU 12.3.20); H42 (Armstrong 5.11.18, sunk in collision with destroyer HMS *Versatile* off Gibraltar 23.2.22); H43 (Armstrong 3.2.19, sold for BU 1944); H44 (Armstrong 17.2.19, sold for BU 1944); H45 (Armstrong, cancelled 1919); H46 (Armstrong, cancelled 1919); H47 (Beardmore 19.11.18, sunk in collision with *L12* 9.7.29); H48 (Beardmore 31.3.19, sold for BU 30.8.35); H49 (Beardmore 15.7.19, sunk by German surface craft off Dutch coast 27.10.40); H50 (Beardmore 25.10.19, sold for BU 1945); H51 (Pembroke DY 15.11.18, sold for BU 6.6.24); H52 (Pembroke DY 31.3.19, sold for BU 9.11.27); H53 (Pembroke DY, cancelled 1919).

'R' CLASS

Displacement: 410 tons surfaced, 503 tons dived.
Dimensions: 49.9m × 4.6m × 3.5m.
Machinery: One shaft, diesel, one electric motor, 240hp/1,200hp for 9.5/15.5 knots. Range 2,000nm at 8 knots surfaced.
Armament: Six 18in bow torpedo tubes, 12 torpedoes.
Complement: 22 officers and men.
R1 (Chatham DY 25.4.18, sold for BU 20.1.23); R2 (Chatham DY 25.4.18, sold for BU 21.2.23); R3 (Chatham DY 8.6.18, sold for BU 21.2.23); R4 (Chatham DY 8.6.18, sold for BU 26.5.34); R5, R6 (both Pembroke DY, laid down

3.18, cancelled 28.8.19); R7 (Vickers 14.5.18, sold for BU 21.2.23); R8 (Vickers 28.6.18, sold for BU 21.2.23); R9 (Armstrong 12.8.18, sold for BU 21.2.23); R10 (Armstrong 5.10.18, sold for BU 19.2.29); R11 (Cammell Laird 16.3.18, sold for BU 21.2.23); R12 (Cammell Laird 9.4.18, sold 21.2.23).

'L' CLASS

Displacement: 891 tons surfaced, 1,074 tons dived.
Dimensions: 70.4m × 17.2m × 4m.
Machinery: Two shafts, diesels, 2 electric motors, 2,400hp/1,600hp for 17/10.5 knots. Range 3,800nm at 10 knots surfaced.

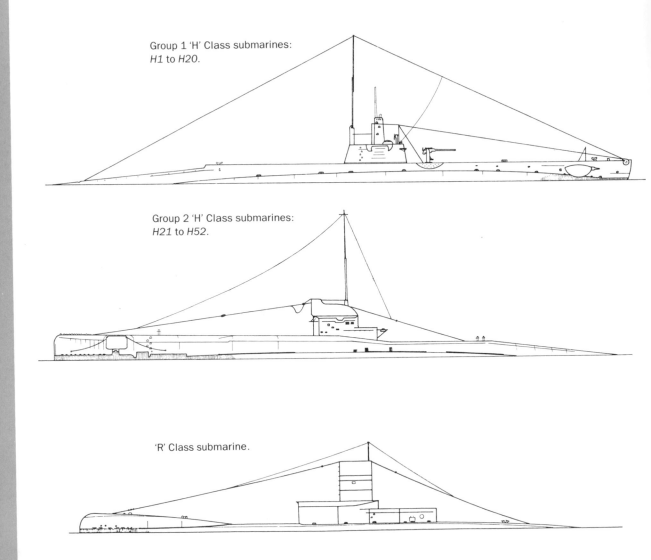

Group 1 'H' Class submarines: H1 to H20.

Group 2 'H' Class submarines: H21 to H52.

'R' Class submarine.

Armament: Six 18in torpedo tubes (four bow, two beam), 10 torpedoes; one 4in gun.

Complement: 35 officers and men.

L1 (ex-*E57*, Vickers 10.5.17, sold for BU 3.30); *L2* (ex-*E58*, Vickers 6.7.17, sold for BU 5.30); *L3* (Vickers 1.9.17, sold for BU 2.31); *L4* (Vickers 17.11.17, sold for BU 24.2.34); *L5* (Swan Hunter 26.1.18, sold for BU 1931); *L6* Beardmore 14.1.18, sold for BU 1.35); *L7* (Cammell Laird 24.4.17, sold for BU 26.2.30); *L8* (Cammell Laird 7.7.17, sold for BU 7.10.30).

L9 CLASS

Displacement: 890 tons surfaced, 1,080 tons dived.

Dimensions: 72.7m × 7.2m × 4m.

Machinery: As 'L' Class.

Armament: Four 21in bow torpedo tubes, 8 torpedoes; two 18in beam torpedo tubes, 2 torpedoes. *L11, L12, L14, L17* and *L25* were not fitted with beam tubes but carried 16 mines (*L25* 14) in vertical chutes in saddle tanks as in 'E' Class. All carried one 4in gun.

Complement: 38 officers and men.

L9 (Denny 29.1.18, foundered at Hong Kong 18.8.23, raised 6.9.23, sold for BU 30.6.27); *L10* (Vickers 24.1.18, war loss 30.10.18); *L11* (Vickers 26.2.18, sold for BU 16.2.32); *L12* (16.3.18, sold for BU 16.2.32); *L14* (Vickers 10.6.18, sold for BU 5.34); *L15* (Fairfield 16.1.18, sold for BU 2.32); *L16* (Fairfield 9.4.18, sold for BU 2.34); *L17* Vickers 13.5.18, sold for BU 2.34); *L18* (Vickers 21.11.18, sold for BU 10.36); *L19* (Vickers 4.2.19, sold for BU 12.4.37); *L20* (Vickers 23.9.18, sold for BU 7.1.35); *L21* (Vickers 11.10.19, sold for BU 2.39); *L22* (Vickers 25.10.19, sold for BU 30.8.35); *L23* (Vickers 1.7.19, foundered in tow to breakers 5.46); *L24* (Vickers 19.2.19, foundered following collision with HMS *Resolution* 10.1.24); *L25* (Vickers 13.2.19, sold for BU 10.35); *L26* (Vickers 29.5.19, sold for BU in Canada 1945); *L27* (Vickers 14.6.19, sold for BU in Canada 1944); *L28–L31* (Vickers, all cancelled 1919); *L32* (Vickers 23.8.1919, not completed,

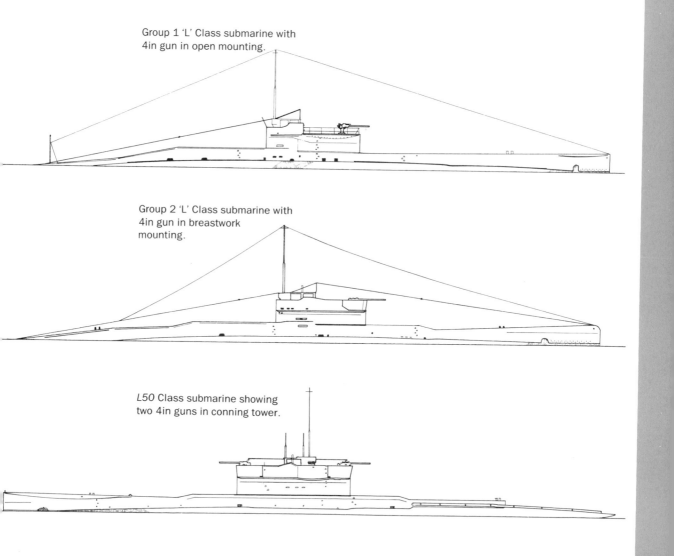

Group 1 'L' Class submarine with 4in gun in open mounting.

Group 2 'L' Class submarine with 4in gun in breastwork mounting.

L50 Class submarine showing two 4in guns in conning tower.

hull sold 1.3.20); *L33* (Swan Hunter 25.9.19, sold 2.32); *L34, L35* (Pembroke DY, both cancelled 1919); *L36* (Fairfield, cancelled 1919); *L37–L49* not ordered.

L50 CLASS

Displacement: 960 tons surfaced, 1,150 tons dived.
Dimensions: 71.6m × 7.2m × 4m.
Machinery: As 'L' Class except endurance 4,500nm at 8 knots surfaced.

Armament: Six 21in bow torpedo tubes, 12 torpedoes; two 4in QF guns.
Complement: 44 officers and men.
L50 (Cammell Laird, cancelled 1.4.19); *L51* (Cammell Laird, cancelled 1919), *L52* (Armstrong 18.12.18, sold for BU 9.35); *L53* (Armstrong 12.8.19, sold for BU 23.1.39); *L54* (Denny 20.8.19, sold for BU 2.2.39); *L55* (Fairfield 21.9.18, mined in Baltic 9.6.19); *L56* (Fairfield 29.5.19, sold for BU 16.4.38); *L57, L58* (Fairfield, cancelled 1.4.19); *L59* (Beardmore, cancelled 1919); *L60, L61*

(Cammell Laird, cancelled 1919); *L62* (Fairfield, cancelled 30.11.18); *L63, L64* (Scotts, cancelled 1919); *L65, L66* (Swan Hunter, cancelled 1919); *L67, L68* (Armstrong, laid down 11.17 and 12.17 respectively, cancelled 1.4.19 and frames used for Yugoslav *Hrabri* and *Nebojsa*); *L69* (Beardmore 6.12.18, sold for BU 2.39); *L70* (Beardmore, cancelled, hull sold 3.20); *L71* (Scotts 17.5.19, sold for BU 25.3.38); *L72* (Scotts, cancelled 1.4.19); *L73* and *L74* (Denny, cancelled 1919).

WAR LOSSES 1914–18

Name	Date	Cause
AE1	19.9.14	Lost off New Britain: cause unknown but suspected ran on to submerged reef.
E3	18.10.14	Torpedoed and sunk off Borkum Island by *U27*.
D5	3.11.14	Mined off Yarmouth.
D2	25.11.14	Lost off Borkum Island.
C31	4.1.15	Presumed mined off Belgian coast.
E10	18.1.15	Presumed mined in Heligoland Bight.
E15	17.4.15	Ran aground while trying to penetrate Dardanelles and abandoned by ship's company. Hull subsequently destroyed by torpedoes fired by British picket boats.
AE2	30.4.15	Scuttled in Sea of Marmara after attack by Turkish *Sultanhissar*.
C33	4.8.15	Presumed mined in North Sea.
E13	19.8.15	Ran aground off Danish coast.
C29	29.8.15	Mined in North Sea.
E7	4.9.15	Scuttled in Dardanelles after being caught in an A/S net.
E20	6.11.15	Torpedoed and sunk in Sea of Marmara by *UB14*.
E6	26.12.15	Mined off Harwich.
E17	6.1.16	Scuttled off Texel after striking submerged rock.
H6	19.1.16	Ran aground off Ameland Island.
E5	7.3.16	Presumed mined off Western Ems.
E24	24.3.16	Presumed mined in North Sea.
E22	25.4.16	Torpedoed and sunk in North Sea by *UB18*.
E18	24.5.16	Lost in Baltic; cause unknown.
E26	3.7.16	Presumed lost off Eastern Ems.
H3	15.7.16	Mined off Cattaro in Adriatic.
B10	9.8.16	Bombed and sunk at Venice by Austrian aircraft while alongside depot ship *Marco Polo*.
E4	15.8.16	Sunk off Harwich in collision with *E41*.
E41	15.8.16	Sunk off Harwich in collision with *E4*.
E16	22.8.16	Lost in North Sea; cause unknown.
E30	22.11.16	Presumed mined off Orford Ness.
E37	1.12.17	Presumed mined in North Sea.
E36	19.1.17	Lost in North Sea, possibly as result of collision with *E43*.
K13	29.1.17	Lost while on trials in Gareloch; salved and renumbered *K22*.

Name	Date	Cause
E49	12.3.17	Mined off Huney Isle, Shetlands.
A10	17.3.17	Sank at Ardrossan after water leaked into ballast tanks.
C16	16.4.17	Sunk off Harwich in collision with HMS *Melampus*.
C34	17.7.17	Torpedoed and sunk east of Fair Isle by *U52*.
E47	20.8.17	Lost in North Sea; cause unknown.
G9	16.9.17	Rammed in error in North Sea by HMS *Pasley*.
C32	22.10.17	Grounded in Vaist Bay, Estonia, and blown up to avoid capture.
K1	18.11.17	Damaged off Danish Coast in collision with *K4*; sunk by HMS *Blanche* to avoid capture.
G8	14.1.18	Lost in North Sea; cause unknown.
H10	19.1.18	Lost in North Sea; cause unknown.
E14	28.1.18	Sunk by gunfire in Dardanelles.
K4	31.1.18	Lost in collision with *K6* in Firth of Forth.
K17	31.1.18	Lost in collision with HMS *Fearless* in Firth of Forth.
E50	1.2.18	Presumed mined in North Sea.
H5	2.3.18	Rammed in error in Irish Sea by SS *Rutherglen*.
D3	12.3.18	Bombed and sunk in error by French airship off Fécamp.
E1	3.4.18	Scuttled in Helsingfors Bay to avoid capture along with *E9* and *E19*.
E8	4.4.18	Scuttled in Helsingfors Bay to avoid capture along with *C26*.
C27	5.4.18	Scuttled in Helsingfors Bay to avoid capture along with *C35*.
C3	23.4.18	Expended during raid on Zeebrugge.
D6	28.6.18	Torpedoed and sunk off Irish Coast by *UB73*.
E34	20.7.18	Lost in North Sea; cause unknown.
L10	3.10.18	Sunk north of Terschelling by gunfire from four German destroyers.
C12	–.10.18	Sunk in harbour accident at Immingham.
J6	15.10.18	Sunk in error by British 'Q' ship *Cymric*.
G7	1.11.18	Lost in North Sea; cause unknown.

42. The crew of *E34* on the casing and conning tower at Harwich, shortly before the submarine was lost in the North Sea on or around 20 July 1918, possibly to a mine. Her CO, Lt R. I. Pulleyne, here on the conning tower, was the only survivor from B2's collision with the *Amerika* in 1912. *E24*, *E34*, *E41*, *E45*, *E46* and *E51* were configured as minelayers carrying twenty mines in ten vertical chutes (two per chute) in the saddle tanks, five on each side of the submarine. Considerable structural modifications were required to fit the mine wells, and the beam torpedo tubes had to be omitted.

43. The engine room of *E34*, showing the two diesel engines which gave the submarine a top speed on the surface of 15 knots. The engines used in the 'E' Class were Vickers four-stroke, eight-cylinder, solid-injection models which gave 800bhp at 380rpm – a total of 1,600bhp. *E3* was fitted with two-stroke, blast-injection engines, which were not successful and were later removed.

▲ 44

▲ 45 ▼ 46

44. *E46* loading mines at Brindisi in 1918. *E46* was the only 'E' Class minelayer to operate outside home waters and laid three fields in the Adriatic off the Dalmatian coast. No ships are recorded as being sunk by her mines; possibly the depth to which they were laid was too great.

45. *E55* on completion. This submarine represented the final stage in the evolution of the 'E' boat design. Improvements in the design included a screen around the conning tower, a large, folding W/T mast (which can be seen at the after end of the casing in the 'down' position), sky searchers on periscopes, sounding machines, Fessenden and water jet signalling gear and, last but no means least, WCs that could be blown at depth. Built by Denny in 1916, *E55* was sold for breaking up in September 1922.

46. The 1912 Submarine Committee recommended that a large boat of about 1,000 tons be built, capable of 20 knots on the surface. However, problems were encountered with the diesel engines: in particular, their ability to develop sufficient power was doubted. Despite these reservations *Nautilus* was ordered in April 1913, detailed work having started much earlier; she is seen here at Barrow. Her construction was a protracted affair and she was not completed until October, having by then abandoned her name in favour of the number *N1*. She saw no operational service, being relegated to training duties. However, *Nautilus* should not be considered a failure for she provided much useful data for future construction.

47. Although the experience with *Nautilus* had been disappointing, the Admiralty persisted with the idea of large submarines and *Swordfish*, shown here in the Clyde on completion, was the second such boat. *Swordfish* was built by Scotts to a design by Laurenti and was driven by steam using a plant originally proposed for *Nautilus*. In the photograph her hydraulically raised funnel can be seen aft of the conning tower but her two 3in guns have not yet been fitted. Her trials were, on the whole, successful, although the large casing meant that water was retained while surfacing, causing her to lose stability. In the end she was converted to a surface patrol boat and broken up in 1922.

48. *G14*, seen here in the Firth of Forth in 1918, was one of fourteen 'G' Class submarines built because of rumours about large German U-boats. A partial double hull was adopted, along with a single stern 21in torpedo tube, although four 18in tubes were fitted forward; the 'Gs' were thus the first RN submarines to carry the 21in torpedo. *G14* was built by Scotts and fitted with Fiat diesels in order to hasten her completion. She was broken up in 1921 but a sister-boat, *G7*, was the last submarine to be sunk in the First World War: the cause of her loss, on or around 1 November 1918, is unknown.

49. *J1* in the basin at Portsmouth on completion. The 'Js' were built in response to the CinC Grand Fleet's requirement for a submarine capable of operating with the fleet. Since Vickers, wrestling with the problems of *Nautilus*'s engines, could not guarantee a high speed on two shafts, the 'Js' became the Royal Navy's only triple-shaft submarines. They had two engine rooms, and machinery occupied 36 per cent of the hull length. Despite early seakeeping problems, which resulted in the bows being raised, the 'Js' proved that they could make 17 knots in the heaviest seas.

47▲

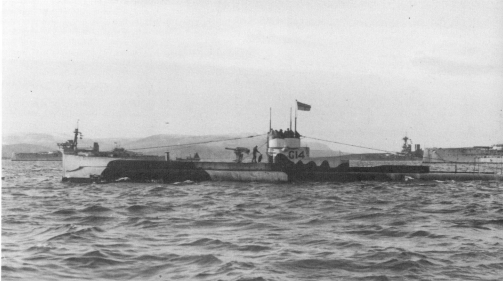

48▲ 49▼

50. Commander Noel Laurence, the first commanding officer of *J1*. On 5 November 1916, while on patrol off Denmark, Laurence encountered units of the High Seas Fleet which were screening the recovery of two U-boats which had gone aground. During the final moments of the attack *J1* lost trim in the heavy swell and Laurence had to fire all four bow tubes before the boat plunged below periscope depth. He was rewarded with two hits, one on the battleship *Kronprinz* under her bridge and the other right aft on her sister the *Grosser Kurfürst*. Both ships were badly damaged, although they returned to harbour under their own steam. Laurence's feat, however, is unique in submarine history: he is the only submariner to hit two capital ships with the same salvo.

51. After her adventures in the North Sea *J1* (now under the command of Lt Cdr Frederick Kennedy) moved to Gibraltar, carrying out anti-submarine patrols in the eastern Atlantic and western Mediterranean where she engaged in an action unique in submarine history – the only one in which one submarine has depth-charged another. *J1* was fitted with depth charges aft and launched them through vertical cylindrical tubes which had outer and inner watertight doors. Once loaded, and with the outer door opened, the charge was literally dropped, *J1* escaping from the effect of the explosion by going at her full speed of 17 knots. Orders for loading and firing were passed from the bridge by means of an engine telegraph type instrument, the actual loading and firing party being under the direction of the Chief Stoker. On 9 November 1918 Kennedy sighted *UB57* and opened fire with his gun. The U-boat promptly dived and *J1* made her historic attack when running over the spot some minutes later.

▲ 50   ▼ 51

52. Four 'J' boats of the 11th Submarine Flotilla at Blyth in 1916. J2 and J3 are the outboard boats, but the identity of the inboard two is unclear. The unusual stovepipe-like structures forward of the conning towers on the nearest 'J' and on J2 are ventilation trunks, most probably for the battery. The photograph clearly shows the great bulk of these large, double-hull submarines.

53. J7 in Plymouth Sound on completion. Built for the Royal Australian Navy J7 had a unique interior layout. The control room was moved 60ft aft so that it lay between the forward and after engine rooms. With the exception of J6, which was sunk in error by the 'Q' ship *Cymeric* on 15 October 1918, the remainder of the class were transferred to the Royal Australian Navy after the war.

54. K6 on builder's trials in Plymouth Sound. The 'K' Class are perhaps the most notorious British submarines ever: of the eighteen boats in the class, eight suffered disasters and there were sixteen major accidents together with an untold number of other mishaps. K6 herself obstinately refused to surface for two hours after a trial dive in a non-tidal basin at Devonport. The 'K' design was prompted by the Grand Fleet's ongoing requirement for a submarine with a high surface speed to work with the Fleet. The role of the 'Ks' would be to scout ahead of the Fleet and break up the enemy's formation with mass torpedo attacks before the start of the main gun engagement, and then finish off the cripples afterwards.

52▲

53▲   54▼

▲55 ▼56

55. *K16* under way and more than justifying the description of a 'K' boat as 'the result of an illicit union between a destroyer and a submarine while no one was looking': early 'Ks' were found to be very wet forward, so the bow was raised as shown in the photograph. *K16* is shown with the modified gun armament of one 12pdr and one 3in arranged aft of the conning tower. It was recognized that the 'Js' were the ultimate in diesel-driven boats: to achieve a high surface speed, steam was the only practical propulsion, and the size of the powerplant dictated the size of the hull.

56. A Thornycroft depth-charge thrower fitted on the after casing of a 'K' boat (possibly *K9*). The fitting of such a weapon, the presence of which must have been the source of considerable unease while the submarine was dived or if it ever came under attack, illustrates the confusion which existed as to how the 'Ks' should be employed: what were the circumstances in which a 'K' boat would use such a weapon?

57. *K22* preparing to dive, with her funnels partially lowered into their wells; this boat once attempted to dive with the funnels raised. With over 40 vent valves involved, diving took a long time (3 minutes 25 seconds was the fastest recorded from full buoyancy, but 5 minutes was the norm, compared with an 'H' boat's 30 seconds) and had to be done carefully so that the tanks were flooded evenly, to avoid a list or longitudinal angle. With a length-to-beam ratio of 12.8:1, the 'Ks' were very difficult to handle when dived and once a bow-down or bow-up angle developed it was difficult to rectify since the broad casing acted as a enormous hydroplane, causing the boat to see-saw. In deep water their unhandiness could prove fatal: a diving depth of 61m and a length of 100.6m meant that the bow could be at crushing depth in seconds if the dive was a steep one. Such was probably the fate of *K5*, lost on 20 January 1921.

57▲

58▲

58. *K22*, undoubtedly the most disaster-prone boat of her class. Built as *K13*, she sank while on trials but was salved and re-named *K22*. On 31 January 1918, while proceeding to sea in company with elements of the Grand Fleet and eight other 'K' boats, she sliced into *K14*, whose helm had jammed while avoiding minesweepers which had not been warned of the Fleet's approach. Minutes later *K22* was rammed by the battlecruiser *Inflexible*. In the resulting confusion *K17* was rammed by the cruiser *Fearless* and *K4* was rammed by *K6* and again by *K7*. *K17* and *K4* sank, but the others returned to Rosyth. The whole affair was known as the Battle of May Island and cost the lives of 103 submariners. There was criticism of the 'K' boats' men by the Admiralty but the correct view, quoted by one of the participants, was that the 'Ks' came to grief because they had the speed of a destroyer, the turning circle of a battlecruiser and the bridge control facilities of a picket boat.

59. *K26* was the ultimate 'K' boat, built to an improved design which included greater flare to the bows to improve seakeeping, a raised superstructure to protect the funnels, repositioned hydroplanes (5m aft, where they would be less susceptible to damage) and the introduction of the 21in torpedo tube for the bow armament. Three were ordered from Armstrong and three from Vickers, but only *K26* was completed. After launch she was towed from Barrow to Chatham and fitted out there at the Royal Dockyard. The photograph clearly shows *K26*'s enhanced gun armament of three 4in.

59▼

▲60

60. *M1*, here displaying her impressive 12in gun, was the product of Admiral 'Jackie'

▼61

Fisher's inventive mind. The gun was intended for action against enemy surface ships, the theory

being that the submarine would come to the surface and loose off one or two rounds before diving;

and for shore bombardment. However, the theory that the gun could be fired while the boat was

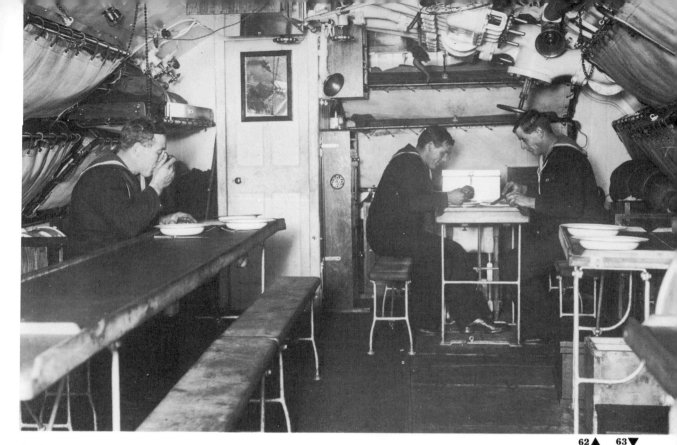

dived with only a portion of the barrel above the water and aiming it with the periscope was flawed, for the gun would be at maximum elevation – implying maximum range – while the view through the periscope would be very limited. *M1* was despatched to the Mediterranean, where plans existed for either a bombardment of the Austrian base at Cattaro or, unbelievably, a passage through the Dardanelles to bombard Constantinople. Fortunately, the war ended before this latter plan could be effected.

61. *M1*'s wardroom, with a genial Commander Max Horton sitting at the table. The great size of the 'M' Class submarines meant that the officers' accommodation was comparatively luxurious. The 'M' boats betrayed none of their 'K' boat ancestry: they were easy to handle, both dived and on the surface, the bulk of the 12in gun helping to take the submarine down while its volume helped to stabilize the boat at periscope depth.

62. The forward mess deck in *M1*. The 'Ms' carried a crew of 65, accommodated in conditions of considerable comfort compared with other submarines. Despite the presence of the bunks, some members of the crew were required to sling hammocks, as indicated on the right of the picture. The 'Ms', or 'Mutton' boats as they were known, were always popular to serve in. *M1* in particular was a very happy boat. Sadly her career ended when she was lost as a result of a collision with the SS *Vidar* on 12 November 1925.

63. *M2* (right) and *M3* looking like two prehistoric monsters; note that *M3* had a cab bridge, designed to give greater shelter, whereas *M2* had an open bridge. *M2* and *M3* were completed after the war and both were soon converted to other roles, the former to a submarine aircraft carrier and the latter to a minelayer. *M2* was lost in an accident off Portland on 26 January 1932 and *M3* was broken up in April 1932.

▲64

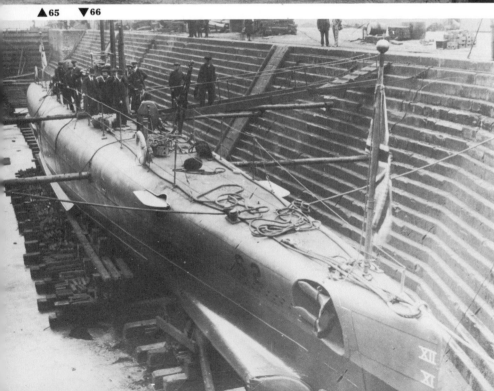

▲65 ▼66

64. *S1* on trials off Greenock. The four 'S' boats were a product of the 1912 Submarine Committee's requirement for a coastal submarine; the same requirement also resulted in the following 'V', 'F' and 'W' classes. *S1* was based on the Italian design by Fiat-San Giorgio and built under licence by Scotts. She was constructed according to the principles of the Italian architect Laurenti, with a double hull, a duck-tail stern and no fewer than ten internal bulkheads (a Group 1 'E' boat had but two).

65. *S1* arriving at Yarmouth on 27 June 1915 under tow by the German trawler *Ost*. The 'S' Class were initially based at Yarmouth and operated in the North Sea. On 21 June 1915, while on patrol ten miles north of Heligoland, *S1* (Lt Cdr Kellett) suffered a port engine failure, followed soon by that of the starboard one. The boat was unable to charge her battery and her prospects looked fairly grim. On 24 June Kellett sighted a German trawler, the *Ost*, and sent over a boarding party. The *Ost* took *S1* in tow and they eventually arrived at Yarmouth, although not before *S1*'s overworked engine staff had had to transfer their attentions to the *Ost*'s machinery.

66. *S2* in dry dock at Scotts. The photograph clearly shows off the ship-shape hull form of these submarines and the arrangement of the two 18in torpedo tubes. The 'S' Class had a high reserve of buoyancy but took a long time to dive – a fault common to many double-hull types. Contrary to some reports, they were sufficiently seaworthy for operations in the North Sea and their transfer to Italy in 1915 was more likely due to the Royal Navy's lack of familiarity with Italian equipment.

67. *V1* was one of a class of four submarines designed and built by Vickers and produced as a rival to the 'S', 'W' and 'F' Class designs; in the climate of experiment prevailing in the RN's submarine service she was accepted. In comparison with other British submarines, the underwater endurance was low, but the 'Vs' fully met all their design requirements. All were broken up after the First World War.

68. *W2* proceeding down the Tyne on completion. The four 'W' boats were built by Armstrong to a French Schneider-Laubeuf design; the French ancestry is very evident in the shape of the hull. After a visit to Toulon the Admiralty concluded against the French design, but four were ordered from Armstrong to fulfil a promise to order two boats (any boats) a year from the company. The first two were armed with two 18in internal tubes as well as four external Drzewiecki drop-collars for launching torpedoes, but the latter were omitted from the second pair. Because of the small diameter of the pressure hull, the boats' habitability was poor but they possessed good handling qualities when dived. As with the 'S' class, they were transferred to Italy in 1916.

69. *F2* on sea trials in the Solent in 1917. The 'Fs' were a class of three built to an Admiralty design for comparison with the 'S'/'W'/'V' types. They were double-hulled and based largely on the 'V' design but with an additional stern tube. *F1* and *F3* had Vickers-type diesels but *F2* had MAN diesels built under licence by Whites. Apart from local defence they saw little war service and were quickly disposed of.

67▲

68▲   69▼

▲70

▲71　▼72

70. The first four 'H' class submarines at St John's, Newfoundland, 17–20 June 1915; *H3* is the outboard boat. As part of the massive wartime expansion programme, the Admiralty ordered ten submarines similar to the US Navy's 'H' Class from Bethlehem Steel, but in order to circumvent the American neutrality laws the boats were to be assembled by Canadian Vickers at Montreal. A second batch of ten boats was ordered direct from Fore River, but the US government warned that the boats could not be delivered until the war was over. In the event the boats were released in 1917 on America's joining the war, but by then the UK 'H' boat programme was under way and, accordingly, six of them were given to Chile as compensation for Chilean warships seized in British yards in 1914.

71. *H1* crossing the Atlantic in 1915 – a journey of record length for any submarine. The 'H' boats were single-hulled and suffered from a low reserve of buoyancy. Note the guard rails fitted along the casing, the tall W/T mast and the extensive canvas screen around the bridge; the figure seated forward of the conning tower is *H1*'s CO, Lt Wilfrid Pirie. *H1* made one patrol in the Sea of Marmara but spent the rest of the war in the Adriatic, where on 16 April 1918 she sank a 'sister' submarine, the Italian *H5*. The Italian boat, also built by Canadian Vickers, was out of her patrol position and had strayed into *H1*'s area.

72. *H4* at Brindisi in 1918. *H1*, *H2*, *H3* and *H4*, later joined by *H7* and *H9*, spent the war in the Adriatic, where *H3* was mined off Cattaro on 15 July 1915. The boats all participated in patrols off the Dalmatian coast, looking for U-boats. Many sightings were made and attacks carried out, including one by *H4* on 28 September 1916, but the target turned out to be a piece of driftwood. *H4* was eventually successful when in a snap night attack on 25 May 1918 she sank *UB52*.

73. *H32*, one of 22 modified 'H' Class submarines built in British yards but to the same design as the Canadian-built 'H' boats. The original programme called for 34 units but was drastically cut back after the Armistice. They were slightly longer than the originals but the main difference was that they were armed with 21in torpedoes as opposed to 18in. Despite the problems inherent in a single-hull design, they were most successful boats and some survived to serve in the Second World War. Note the improved bridge, giving greater protection than that fitted to *H4*.

74. Inside an 'H' boat under construction, looking forward from aft. The apertures for the four bow 21in torpedo tubes are clearly visible at the end of the boat. The workmen in the midships portion of the boat are working on the battery section: because of the single-hull design

the main and auxiliary ballast tanks were placed under and beside the battery tanks, where their tops extended well above the battery tanks, as can be seen in the photograph.

73▲

74▼

▲ 75

75. *R2*, one of a class of eight submarines designed specifically for hunting U-boats and unique in that their submerged speed was greater than their speed on the surface. The design was years ahead of its time and was not without its problems: a diving depth of 45m, a top underwater speed of 15 knots and hydroplanes controlled by hand through rod and chain gearing meant that life in an 'R' boat could be exciting.

▼ 76

76. The business end of *R8*, showing her six 18in torpedo tubes. Apart from *K26*, the 'R' Class carried the heaviest bow torpedo armament of any British submarine of the First World War. There was provision for the stowage of six reload torpedoes, but this must have been most difficult and would have been at the expense of some of the accommodation. The wooden cabinet on the port side aft of the tube space contained the hydrophone equipment – an unusually comprehensive array of five hydrophones, with which, it was claimed, the boat could track a target without using the periscope. *R8* was the only one of the class to have a chance of attacking a U-boat in October 1918, but the torpedo did not run straight.

77. *R4* was the last of the class to survive: she served in a training role at Portland and was not broken up until 1934. Her nickname of 'Slug' testifies to her streamlined form for high underwater speed, although the single screw made manoeuvring on the surface difficult.

78. *L8* on completion. The 'L' Class marked a return to the saddle-tank hull-form after all the experiments with single and double hulls. The 'Ls' were really the true successors to the 'E' Class design; they were larger and faster but, in *L1–L8*, retained the 18in torpedo. All the boats carried a gun on the forward casing: a 4in was eventually fitted but in the meantime a variety of weapons were mounted, *L1*, for example having a 3in on a 'disappearing' HA mounting. Here *L8* is not carrying a gun, although the platform is clearly visible.

79. *L6*, showing the revised position of the gun on a raised platform, with a separate access trunk forward of the conning tower. The gun is here placed in an open mounting but was later incorporated into a breastwork mounting.

77▲

78▲　79▼

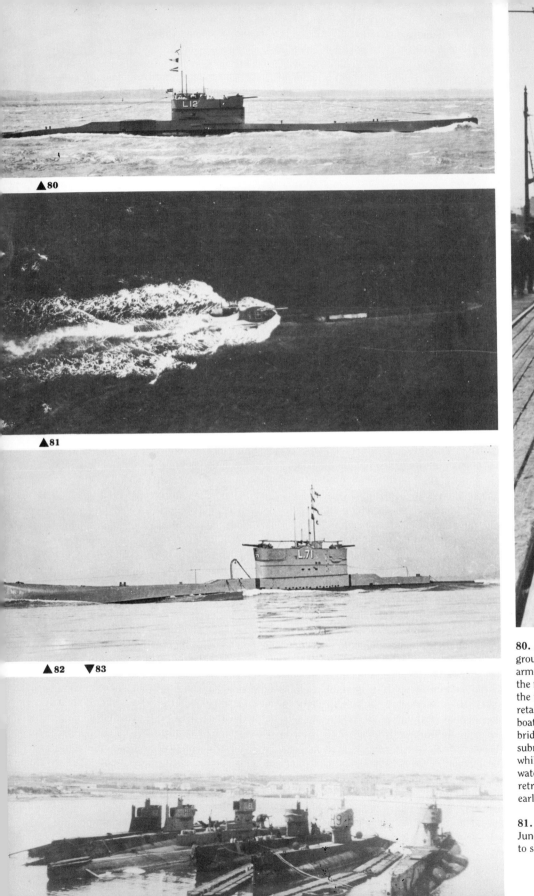

▲80

▲81

▲82 ▼83

80. *L12* was one of the second group of 'L' boats which were armed with the 21in torpedo for the forward armament, although the two 18in beam tubes were retained. In *L12* and subsequent boats the 4in gun was raised to bridge level in order that the submarine could engage a target while lying trimmed down in the water, and this modification was retrospectively carried out to the earlier boats.

81. *L10* diving during trials in June 1918 which were intended to show the visibility or other-

wise at various depths of a dived submarine. The gun is just awash but the outline of the hull can be plainly seen. L10 was the only member of her class to be lost during the First World War, being sunk by gunfire from four German destroyers off Terschelling on 3 October 1918. The destroyers *S33*, *S34*, *V28* and *V29* were on patrol when *S34* struck a mine and sank. While rescuing the crew *S33* was also hit, but thoughts that she too had been mined were dispelled when *L10* broached, doubtless because she lost trim after firing

at 5.33. The German ships lost no time in opening fire and *L10* was hit several times, sinking with no survivors.

82. *L71* was an *L50* Class submarine which carried a second aft-facing 4in gun and six bow 21in torpedo tubes while omitting the beam 18in tubes. The *L50*s were ordered before any experience had been gained with the 'L' Class, and they experienced considerable problems. The speed was low: no more than 14 knots could be achieved, although the

designers had hoped for 17.5 knots. The class also experienced stability problems caused by the great size of the conning tower.

83. British submarines at the end of the First World War: 'Rotten Row' in Grand Harbour, Malta, showing the workhorses of the Mediterranean Fleet awaiting disposal. From left to right are *H2*, *H4*, *E11* (in which Nasmith won the VC), *H1*, *H9* and *E2*.

84. Three submarines alongside at Fort Blockhouse illustrate the state of British submarine development at the end of the

First World War, after all the experiments with double-hull and fleet submarines. Inboard is *L12*, an overseas saddle-tank patrol submarine; in the centre is *H28*, a coastal, single-hull submarine; while outboard is *R7*, designed specially for anti-submarine operations. The 'L' and 'H' Classes would form the mainstay of the postwar fleet but the 'R' Class would soon be discarded.

The *Fotofax* series

A new range of pictorial studies of military subjects for the modeller, historian and enthusiast. Each title features a carefully-selected set of photographs plus a data section of facts and figures on the topic covered. With line drawings and detailed captioning, every volume represents a succinct and valuable study of the subject. New and forthcoming titles:

Warbirds
F-111 Aardvark
P-47 Thunderbolt
B-52 Stratofortress
Stuka!
Jaguar
US Strategic Air Power:
  Europe 1942–1945
Dornier Bombers
RAF in Germany

Vintage Aircraft
German Naval Air Service
Sopwith Camel
Fleet Air Arm, 1920–1939
German Bombers of WWI

Soldiers
World War One: 1914
World War One: 1915
World War One: 1916
Union Forces of the American
  Civil War
Confederate Forces of the
  American Civil War
Luftwaffe Uniforms
British Battledress 1945–1967
  (2 vols)

Warships
Japanese Battleships, 1897–
  1945
Escort Carriers of World War
  Two
German Battleships, 1897–
  1945
Soviet Navy at War, 1941–1945
US Navy in World War Two,
  1943–1944
US Navy, 1946–1980 (2 vols)
British Submarines of World
  War One

Military Vehicles
The Chieftain Tank
Soviet Mechanized Firepower
  Today
British Armoured Cars since
  1945
NATO Armoured Fighting
  Vehicles
The Road to Berlin
NATO Support Vehicles

The *Illustrated* series

The internationally successful range of photo albums devoted to current, recent and historic topics, compiled by leading authors and representing the best means of obtaining your own photo archive.

Warbirds
US Spyplanes
USAF Today
Strategic Bombers, 1945–1985
Air War over Germany
Mirage
US Naval and Marine Aircraft
  Today
USAAF in World War Two
B-17 Flying Fortress
Tornado
Junkers Bombers of World War
  Two
Argentine Air Forces in the
  Falklands Conflict
F-4 Phantom Vol II
Army Gunships in Vietnam
Soviet Air Power Today
F-105 Thunderchief
Fifty Classic Warbirds
Canberra and B-57
German Jets of World War Two

Vintage Warbirds
The Royal Flying Corps in
  World War One
German Army Air Service in
  World War One
RAF between the Wars
The Bristol Fighter
Fokker Fighters of World War
  One
Air War over Britain, 1914–
  1918
Nieuport Aircraft of World War
  One

Tanks
Israeli Tanks and Combat
  Vehicles
Operation Barbarossa
Afrika Korps
Self-Propelled Howitzers
British Army Combat Vehicles
  1945 to the Present
The Churchill Tank
US Mechanized Firepower
  Today
Hitler's Panzers
Panzer Armee Afrika
US Marine Tanks in World War
  Two

Warships
The Royal Navy in 1980s
The US Navy Today
NATO Navies of the 1980s
British Destroyers in World
  War Two
Nuclear Powered Submarines
Soviet Navy Today
British Destroyers in World
  War One
The World's Aircraft Carriers,
  1914–1945
The Russian Convoys, 1941–
  1945
The US Navy in World War
  Two
British Submarines in World
  War Two
British Cruisers in World War
  One
U-Boats of World War Two
Malta Convoys, 1940–1943

Uniforms
US Special Forces of World
  War Two
US Special Forces 1945 to the
  Present
The British Army in Northern
  Ireland
Israeli Defence Forces, 1948 to
  the Present
British Special Forces, 1945 to
  Present
US Army Uniforms Europe,
  1944–1945
The French Foreign Legion
Modern American Soldier
Israeli Elite Units
US Airborne Forces of World
  War Two
The Boer War
The Commandos World War
  Two to the Present
Victorian Colonial Wars

A catalogue listing these series and other Arms & Armour Press titles is available on request from: Sales Department, Arms & Armour Press, Artillery House, Artillery Row, London SW1P 1RT.